D0760062

Dancing in the Emp

∾

Dancing in the Empty Spaces

Meditations

David O. Rankin

Skinner House Books

BOSTON

Printed in Canada

Cover design by Suzanne Morgan
Text design by Sandra Rigney

ISBN 1-55896-413-4

Library of Congress Cataloging-in-Publication Data

Rankin, David O., 1937–
  Dancing in the empty spaces : meditations / by David O. Rankin.
     p. cm.
  ISBN 1-55896-413-4 (alk. paper)
   1. Meditations. 2. Unitarian Universalists—Prayer-books and
devotions—English. I. Title.

BV4832.2 .R33 2000
242—dc21   00-049257

10 9 8 7 6 5 4 3 2 1
04 03 02 01 00

Love is the sum of all theology.

Table of Contents

Preface

As a fair disclosure, I must confess to a multitude of
personal weaknesses. I cannot sing a song, bake a pie,
draw a picture, or change a fluorescent lightbulb. I
flunked trigonometry twice, and I have still not found it
anywhere in the real world. My mother thought I would
be an outstanding doctor, because no one could read my
writing.

But I did have a limited range of abilities, including
the capacity to appreciate the magical power of language.
Even today, I enjoy being locked in a room, stringing
words together, and listening to the rhythms of various
combinations—which is no way for a grown-up to
behave.

Dancing in the Empty Spaces is the product of thirty
years of disciplined meditation. It presents a variety of
topics, but is purposely diverse, nonlinear, and devoid of
ultimate resolutions. Like Zen, it revels in the mystery
of paradox and celebrates the intensity of the present
moment. I hope each piece leads to further thought,
since the search for truth is truly never-ending.

David O. Rankin

Dancing in the Empty Spaces

∾

All life is a paradox: a blended soup of changing ideas, a subtle balance of conflicting needs, a fragile alliance of opposing values. The world is a process, a mystery, an impossibility. Limited in our perceptions, and born into an infinitely evolving universe, we are creatures of sheer ambiguity, who grow only through enduring the tension and exploring the boundaries of the unknown. So let us dance in the empty spaces, be nimble and be quick, for we are on an odyssey that lasts forever.

Existence

Genuine existence is the courageous encounter with the world, strained through the pores of the five senses, and involving us as partners in a continuous creation. It is an ongoing process, and the process itself is the actuality, since no sooner do we arrive than we start on a fresh adventure.

Waking Up!

~

How often I want to shout:

"Every moment is a sacred moment!" To grab people, turn them around, upside down, and pull them out of mundaneness, screaming, "Every moment is a sacred moment!"

For it will not come again.

Freedom

Freedom is the ground of all vital activity. Faith without freedom is dogma. Love without freedom is an illusion. Justice without freedom is oppression. In every instance, freedom is the factor that sustains and completes the other goal. It is the oxygen of the human spirit, the indispensable element for growth and wholeness.

Aging

~

Have you ever attended a class reunion?

After several years, you are suddenly thrust with men and women your own age. You approach someone you hardly recognize, and you say to yourself:

> "What a sight!"

> "How he has changed!"

> "Is that the lithe tennis player?"

> "What a shipwreck he has become!"

Looking around, you see that everyone has been altered. It is like a costume ball, where you are merely a spectator, watching the figures from another era.

Luckily, you have not obeyed the same laws as those other people. Time has passed for them, but quite mercifully spared you. Going home, you congratulate yourself on being the only member of the class who is still recognizable.

Of course, everyone else is doing the same.

Poetry

The poet is concerned with economy and precision:
explaining the universe in a word, squeezing each vowel
for an ultimate meaning, and arranging the empty
spaces for the eye to sink in mystery. It is engaging the
meaninglessness and silence of time until they are forced
to mean, until the silence answers, and until the
nonbeing is *being*.

Being Human

≈

To be human is to be in touch with the larger
rhythms and harmonies of the universe;

To be human is to be aware of the beauty of a
creation that continually unfolds;

To be human is to be the servants of the earth
upon which our existence depends;

To be human is to embrace the present moment
as a sacred, joyful occasion;

To be human is to nurture bridges of intimacy
that are global and inclusive;

To be human is to be in a state of process: to
live, to love, and to never die.

Progress

~

My first clock was a pocket watch, with a large, round face, bold numbers, and three sweeping hands for hours, minutes, and seconds. It was a captivating piece of machinery. Then I bought a new wristwatch, with a small, flat face, no numbers, and only two tiny hands for hours and minutes. It was the very latest development in clock technology. Now I am the owner of a digital watch, with no face, flashing numbers, and no hands for hours, minutes, and seconds. In other words, the clock has almost totally disappeared.

Obviously, the telling of time has "progressed" in terms of speed, efficiency, and convenience, but it is no longer a great visual adventure or a unique aesthetic pleasure. With the old pocket watch, I could feel the movement, scan the entire day, hear the brutal ticking of the seconds, and ponder the meaning of the passage of time. Also, I was personally responsible for winding and correcting the instrument, an active participant in the process of marking the turning of the earth.

With the advent of "progress," I only see some luminous numerals, entirely divorced from thought and feeling, a dull, precise reminder of the present moment.

The Spiritual Journey

~

In the pulpit, I cannot preach bromides: If it is easy, it is probably false; if it is popular, it is soon outmoded; if it is soothing, it is lacking depth; if it is final, it is clearly dead—and what remains is the rigorous journey, which demands the highest degree of dogged persistence.

It is Moses leading the Jews through the desert of Sinai, and Jesus enduring the temptations in the wilderness of Israel, and Buddha seeking enlightenment along the dusty roads of India.

It is the glorious voyage of Odysseus in Homer's *Odyssey*, the narrow paths through the circles of hell in Dante's *Inferno*, and the confessions of the travelers in Chaucer's *Canterbury Tales*.

It is the pilgrims sailing on the *Mayflower*, the settlers moving westward, being *On the Road* with Jack Kerouac, and spinning through a black hole in Kubrick's *2001: A Space Odyssey*.

Whatever the specific goal: a battle for honor, a ritual of passage, a quest for the grail, a return to Eden, a search for identity, a pilgrimage to Mecca, or a visit to the land of Oz, there is always the higher journey toward spiritual fulfillment—of rebirth, renewal, and transfiguration.

Honoring Thy Father

~

When I was eight years old, he hit me in the face with a pork chop for talking back to his wife. But he was the gentlest man I have ever known.

When I was nine years old, he encouraged me to learn to defend myself on the streets. But he could always wrestle me to the ground with one arm.

When I was ten years old, I informed him that I was going to run away from home. He offered to buy me a bus ticket and told me to take a winter jacket.

When I was eleven years old, he announced it was time I work for a living. I was employed as a golf ball retriever, but he never recommended a particular career.

When I was fifteen years old, he presented the first and only lecture on sex education. It was only one brief sentence, somewhat muffled, unspeakably graphic, and forever useful.

When I was eighteen years old, he shook my hand and sent me off to college. I was thereafter known as one of those "damn college kids!"

When I was twenty years old, he told me I could have a car, if I bought it with my own money, paid all the bills, and promised not to cruise around.

When I was twenty-one years old, he took me to his favorite tavern and bought me a beer. We talked about baseball and politics but never returned.

When I was twenty-three years old, he wrote me a letter on the presidential election. It was one of the few times he ever asked me a real question—or sought my advice.

A few months later, he died.

He was my father, but I never knew him well.

The Meek Inherit the Earth

Lucille was a long-time member of the church, an extremely shy and humble individual. When I visited her at the hospital, I learned she was suffering from leukemia. We talked for a short time, although she was very weak.

As I tiptoed from the room, she said in a soft voice, "I have not completed my pledge to the church." Surprised by the comment, I replied, "Don't you worry. It can certainly wait. I'll see you in the morning." She died that night.

But sometime during the evening hours, between the moment I left the room and the moment she died, Lucille had managed to get out of bed. She made her way to a dresser in the corner of the room. She found a pen and a checkbook.

With a shaking hand, she wrote a check to the church she loved for many years. I found it in the mail the day after her death, the last communication of a tidy soul. It was the most memorable pledge I have ever received.

Yes, Maybe

∾

After a worship service, I was greeting people in the reception line.

"Congratulations," she said. "You read his poetry very well."

"Thank you," I replied.

"Of course, he was not always a happy man," she continued. "His life was a struggle. Hope was hard won. Even in the end, if he affirmed anything at all, it was a yes, maybe."

"You seem to know a lot about him," I said.

"Not everything," she replied. "But I am his daughter."

It was 1974, the one hundredth anniversary of his birth. We were talking about Robert Frost.

If you are a "yes" type of person, you may not understand Robert Frost. He does not speak well to the once-born, to the buoyant and optimistic, to those who are blessed with a happy hope and a cheerful faith.

If you are a "no" type of person, you may not understand Robert Frost. He does not speak well to the life-denying, to the cynical or nihilistic, to those who lack a candle of hope and a spark of faith.

But if you are on the edge, a "yes, maybe" type of person—wrestling with the inner demons, searching to find the meaning of life, clinging with your fingernails to a dim hope and a fragile faith—then you will understand Robert Frost. He is your Advent poet.

Waving the Palms

~

Palm Sunday is found:

whenever we are serving a noble and unpopular
cause with selfless devotion, holding to the ideals
of truth and justice;

whenever we are seeking to uplift the fallen, to
comfort the brokenhearted, to strengthen and
encourage the weak and hopeless;

whenever we are working bravely and persistently
in the face of abuse and criticism to establish more
equitable relations in the world;

whenever we are sacrificing our lives in behalf of
what we believe to be the service of love for all
humanity.

That is Palm Sunday!

Church and State

~

I believe in the art of politics:
    to improve conditions,
    to assure self-government,
    to maintain a democratic society.
But I also believe in the spirit of religion:
    to be free,
    to stir the conscience,
    to breathe without the chains of oppression.

I believe in the vocation of politicians:
    to make peace,
    to effect compromise,
    to smooth the pursuit of happiness.
But I also believe in the calling of clergy:
    to seek truth,
    to serve the highest,
    to spread the gospel of liberation.

I believe in the power of the state:
    to combat crime,
    to encourage education,
    to devise projects of mutual assistance.
But I also believe in the mission of the church:
    to embody love,
    to side with the weak,
    to awaken the hearts of people.

Talking to Myself

~

First, I must begin with my own creation. I must celebrate the miracle of evolution that resulted in a living entity named David. I must assist in the unfolding of the process by deciding who I am, by fashioning my own identity, by creating myself each day. I must listen to the terrors, the desires, the impulses that clash in the depths of my soul. I must know myself, or I will be made and used by others.

Second, I must learn to affirm my neighbor. I must respect others, not for their function, but for their *being*. I must put others at the center of my attention, to treat them as ends, and to recognize our common destiny. I must never use people to win glory, or to measure the ego, or to escape from responsibility. I must listen to their words, their thoughts, their coded messages.

Finally, I must value action more than intention. I must feel, think, judge, decide, and then risk everything in acts of gratuitous freedom. I must batter the walls of loneliness. I must leap the barriers of communication. I must tear down the fences of anonymity. I must destroy the obstacles to life and liberty. Not in my mind (as a wistful dream), but in my acts (as a daily reality).

Natural Theology

~

Is there such a thing as God?

    I saw a sunrise at Jackson Hole.

    I fell in love many years ago.

    I caught a tear in my father's eye.

    I watched a lily bloom.

    I saved a boy from drugs and death.

    I touched the hand of Martin Luther King, Jr.

    I feel the warmth of children.

    I laugh almost every day.

    I hold the hem of hope.

The only God I can possibly know is the God of life—
and life is endless.

Politics in the Pulpit

~

In 1968, I delivered a sermon prior to the presidential election. It was not a partisan plea, since I was not overly impressed with either Richard Nixon or Hubert Humphrey.

Instead, I merely recommended, at the conclusion of the sermon, that I hoped everyone would vote for the most intelligent, experienced, and compassionate candidate.

So imagine my surprise when a man confronted me in the reception line and angrily shouted, "How dare you use the pulpit to support Hubert Humphrey!"

Trust

When I trust:

I am able to engage in the process of discovering who I am and of creating what I will become.

I am able to function honestly and naturally without masks, defenses, and deceptions.

I am able to reveal hidden desires and inner weaknesses without fear of criticism.

I am able to focus on constructive projects rather than brooding over imagined wrongs.

I am able to join in authentic relationships, in intimate sharing, and in personal dialogue.

I am able to appreciate the nature of others for what they do and what they are.

I am able to act in freedom with little regard for status, power, authority, or manipulation.

I am able to take risks, sail on fresh adventures, and explore the dark regions of the world.

I am able to touch the springs of consciousness and to see the inherent potential of life.

Trust is saying "*Yes*" to creation.

Letting Go

≈

If we cannot let go, we cannot survive. Letting go is freedom, autonomy, and emancipation.

When people hold on to an old faith, simply out of lazy habit and hoary tradition, as it does nothing for the growth of the spirit or the nurturing of the mind, burying their soul in a pit of irrelevance—they should be letting go.

When people hold on to biases or prejudices, lies inherited in childhood, that restrict their vision of humanity, spreading pain and suffering to the innocent victims of a distorted perception of reality—they should be letting go.

When people hold on to destructive relationships or dependence on drugs, abuse, anger, domination, or arrangements of mutual convenience, which demean them and damage their characters—they should be letting go.

When people hold on to the images of youth with makeup and facelifts, unbuttoned shirts and long gold chains, trying to relive a wasted adolescence, while ignoring the challenges of wisdom and maturity—they should be letting go.

When people hold on to the grief of a death, sleeping with the ghosts of the past, embracing the demons of remorse, and refusing to walk in the sunshine, where the light leads to growth, happiness, and God—they should be letting go.

Let us heed the encouragement, to have, to hold, and, in time, to let go!

The Edge

~

A religion that promises a life without tension, a life without conflict, a life without suffering, is a religion of passivity, a religion of mediocrity, a religion of insignificance. Everything worth doing in the world is a desperate gamble, a game of chance, where nothing is certain.

What is love? Is it not a wild and sublime speculation that can end in ecstasy or despair?

What is courage? Is it not a hazardous risk of fortune that can end in victory or defeat?

What is adventure? Is it not a blind leap in the dark that can end in joy or disaster?

What is faith? Is it not a prayerful flip of the coin that can end in heaven or hell?

If I refuse to play the game, if I refuse to risk myself, if I refuse to throw the dice, I am never really alive. I am then only flesh, baking in the sun on a middling plateau, with no view of the valley and no road to the peak.

Jazz

∿

My favorite artists have no rigid structure. Their works display a complex interplay of opposing forces:

order and turmoil,

fate and freedom,

light and darkness,

emotion and thought,

the spiritual and the physical.

These are the images of tension, of a seesaw, of a pendulum, that I find in the real world. They are why I prefer jazz, which requires a creative, moment-to-moment improvisation—a dialectical response to a paradoxical reality.

Religion

~

I do not agree with those who say that you must believe only in God, or Jesus, or Muhammad, or the Book of Mormon, or Dr. Sun Myung Moon, in order to be a religious person. You are religious because you are a person. You are religious because you are a conscious and reflective human being. You are religious because you are required, even forced, by your very nature, to frame a response to the ultimate questions of life. There is no escape! Religion is a given, an inherited condition of a singular species that needs a structure of meaning.

Death

~

My ministry to the dying, though filled with tears, has been a trial worth enduring.

I have learned that a single human life is the most precious entity in all of God's creation, not to be bartered for a genie's wish or a king's fortune.

I have learned that our abundant existence on earth is too much filled with petty thoughts, trivial concerns, and a meanness toward our fellow creatures.

I have learned that it is good to live with a knowledge of our finitude, as if each moment is our last, so that what we do is a new kind of doing.

I have learned that the fear of death, which arises from our personal fantasies and cultural anxieties, is more to be dreaded than death itself.

And I have also learned that the human being is a marvelous construction, with the faith and courage to confront any power in the universe—even the reaper, whose name is Death.

Creativity

~

Creativity is a natural endowment, a potential with which we are born, like taste, or sight, or hearing. It is a marvelous gift.

Creativity is the recognition that the energy and freshness of childhood can be re-experienced in adulthood. It is always present.

Creativity is listening to the inner voice, with an appreciation of our own uniqueness and individuality. It is self-understanding.

Creativity is the acceptance of teachers and significant events in our lives that help us to grow in wisdom. It is welcoming insights.

Creativity is evolving with the head and heart together, being available to ourselves at every level of life. It is personal integration.

Creativity is knowing the ugly parts of ourselves as well as the beautiful, the wild as well as the controlled. It is self-criticism.

Creativity is daring to challenge the popular authorities, the haughty defenders of antiquated truths. It is an old rugged cross.

Silence

Silence is not always golden. Sometimes, silence is a contempt for goodness; silence is a consent for atrocities; silence is a scorn for humanity. Often, it is better to scream.

Belief and Action

~

It is not enough to believe in God, even with the purest doctrine, the ideal creed, and the highest devotion—to the point where we are nominated for sainthood.

Instead, we must express our faith in explicit action: in building paths to effective remedies, in structuring a better society, in responding to the perils of our time.

It is not enough to believe in the grace of God, to wait, to sit back, and to depend on a bolt from heaven—no matter how firm, or trusting, or confident we feel in our faith.

Instead, we must act in the absence of God: seeking out the needy, identifying injustice, risking controversy, knocking on the door of failure, but walking steadily toward Jerusalem.

It is not enough to worship, pray, and bow down, as if offerings will purchase heaven, as if meditations will alleviate hunger, as if hymns will still the cries of the poor.

Instead, we must stress the primacy of love over piety, the primacy of service over servility, the primacy of sympathy over a safe, timid, and smothering obedience to an old ritual.

Doubt

~

An honest "No" is a glorious statement.

Doubt is the expression of faith in the intelligence and imagination of humanity.

Doubt is the expression of humility about the capacity for errors and mistakes.

Doubt is the expression of wisdom when popular and rewarding truths are wrong.

Doubt is the expression of confidence that knowledge can always be improved.

Doubt is the expression of courage in confronting the dangerous and destructive.

Doubt is the expression of hope that a better world is waiting for the future.

Doubt is the expression of harmony with the unceasingly changing universe.

Doubt is the expression of concern for the proper integration of thought and experience.

It is not evil, but good, an intrinsic element of faith.

Time

Time does nothing! It is an empty vessel, waiting to be filled with something and capable of being filled with anything.

Time does not tell—we tell.

Time does not cure—we cure.

Time does not drag—we drag.

Stop cheering or blaming time, when we are the heroes or the villains! The vessel is ours to pour into, and the drink, sour or sweet, is our own concoction.

Sunday Morning

~

I declare a Sabbath Day—to walk in the wilderness of enlarged perceptions;

I declare a release from work—to nourish the stamina to pursue ideals;

I declare a special hour—to help cherish life's joys and combat life's sorrows;

I declare a reign of holiness—to deepen our grounding in the sustaining mystery.

I declare a time for simply being and letting go, for rediscovering great, forgotten truths, for basking in the arts of the ages, and for learning how to live again.

Believing

~

I believe in the Holy,
    lifting, sustaining,
    among us, within us,
    around us.

I believe in Living,
    with a song to sing,
    in awe, in adoration,
    out of joy, out of praise.

I believe in Loving,
    in intimate communion,
    of gentle compassion,
    and the giving of roses.

I believe in Seeking,
    daring to explore,
    doubting without fear,
    cautious in certainties.

I believe in Prophecy,
    the spirit of outrage,
    clapping like thunder,
    healing the world.

The Blues

~

I love listening to the blues. It is strangely comforting. It is a form of therapy. Have you ever listened? Really listened?

It begins by confronting a reality.

It presents the feelings of despair.

It explores the hurts and discords.

It searches for viable alternatives.

It does not settle for easy solutions.

It roams up the alleys and dead ends.

It probes down into the darkest void.

It gropes along through the emptiness.

It comes upon a buried, forgotten truth.

It takes delight in the essential discovery.

It lifts the spirit on the wings of a new harmony!

I love the blues. It is an honest musical tradition. It is a form of salvation. Have you ever sung? Really sung?

"If that's all there is my friends,
        then let's keep dancing . . ."

Perception

~

I am 27 years old. I was thinking about it the other day. It is very interesting.

I have always been 27 years old. When people said I was 9 years old, and 12 years old, and 19 years old, I knew they were wrong. I was a tall, slim, 27-year-old man with dark brown hair, my own gray sport coat, and imported beer in the refrigerator. I was never a boy or an adolescent. I do not know why people were confused. I knew what I was.

I will always be 27 years old. If people say I am 30 years old, and 45 years old, and 63 years old, I know they are wrong. I am a tall, slim, 27-year-old man with dark brown hair, two gray sport coats, and a bottle of Alka-Seltzer in the cupboard. I will never be middle-aged or a senior citizen. I do not know why people are joking. I know what I am.

I was once shown a picture (said to be of me) of a little boy. He was a skinny little runt with a silly smile and tennis shoes. Who would ever have wanted to be that little boy? Not me! As long as I live, I will be 27 years old, even though parents, teachers, and the police have treated me like a younger person. They did not know my age.

Last week, a man on the television (with my name) looked very old. There was gray on his hair and not on his coat. He was not so slim. Who would ever want to grow up like that? Not me! I am fortunate for being only 27 years old—no matter what happens in the outside world. People do not see everything. What do they know? I know what I will always be.

I learned yesterday that Ginger, my wife, is 19 years old. She has always been 19 years old. She said so herself. I am glad to be a little older. We will never change. How old are you?

Mind and Soul

∾

The ideal religion is a combination of the head and the heart.

If your religion is only a rational construction, it will stiffen into a dry, meatless, and unappealing bone. Faith without sensation is arid.

If your religion is only a spiritual perception, it will degenerate into a muddy swamp of obscure gibberish. Faith without reason is mush.

The proper balance is what William James described as "the union of the mathematician with the poet, fervor with measure, passion with correctness, this surely is the ideal."

Simple Pleasures

~

I prefer the modest joys, the understated incarnations, the distilled moments of simple pleasure that are sneaky blessings to everyone:

the capacity to play and to be renewed by a restful sleep, the whole range of tastes from sweet to bitter and the mysteries in between, the delicate slender fingers of an infant child, the color of sky and sea and the vast complex of hues that melt through the eyes, the sheer wonder of sound shaking the inner soul with tones of depths and heights, the tender remembrance of times that were good and whole, the rustic places that lunged out and lodged in the heart, the persons who shared their secret loves in moments beyond all measuring, the coming of day and the sureness of the return of night, the loyalty of a pet when humans forget to care, the aloneness of solitude that stirs the mind in new directions, the muted meanings that each of us finds in the cycle of life and that hold fast through the fearful rhythms, and all of the subtle and lumbering awarenesses that pulse in us—

for which our hearts sing their joyful "Amen!"

Advent

∾

During the Advent season, we celebrate the qualities of faith, hope, love, and joy. Yet these must be viewed through the prism of paradox.

No Faith is worthy without the capacity to doubt all things—for then it is only credulity.

No Hope is possible without the specter of defeat in the wings—for then it is only dreaming.

No Love is strong without the dread of loss in the heart—for then it is only passion.

No Joy is complete without the certainty of sorrow in the future—for then it is only frivolity.

Thus, it is wrong to mislead people with simplistic notions, for they distract us from the fullness of life. After all, the seas have storms, the clouds have lightning, and the roses have thorns—forever.

The Joy of Christmas

~

It might be a joy of long ago:
> your first white tennis shoes, baking a cake with your
> mother, sliding down a hill on a sled, a gift from the
> tooth fairy, or the A on a spelling exam.

It might be a joy of recognition:
> a face across a crowded room, holding hands in the
> woods, the father you finally understand, a friendship
> that has never died, or saying, "I like myself!"

It might be a joy of victory:
> standing in a graduation line, advancing in a career,
> a year of sobriety, watching the children grow in
> wisdom and sensitivity, or losing an inch around the
> middle.

It might be a joy of legend:
> the birth of a child, a star in the sky, the promise of
> peace, gifts from strangers, and all the elements of
> cheer that appeared in a stable in Bethlehem—lifting
> the hearts in great rejoicing.

Joy is the keynote of Christmas.

Palm Sunday

∼

I am a Palm Sunday Christian,
    waving the palm for freedom.
Always the roots need to be exposed.
Always the chains need to be broken.
Always the rulers need to be shaken.

To wave the palm implies a vision
    of the world
Nearer to the heart's desire,
A faith that it shall be,
And a readiness to pay the price
    of failure.

Even in victory,
    with friends parading in the streets,
    drunk with the taste of success,
I will stand on the curb
    with the palm still waving,
    as a warning and a judgment.

Easter Morning

∿

Dear God:

Good Friday is gone—a dark day on the calendar,
A time of suffering—with more losses than gains,
And more pain than we thought we could bear.

    We are tired of crying,

    We are tired of burying,

    We are tired of mourning.

But Easter is here—and we who survived are prepared
For the turning of the year—not to escape the past,
But to provide a witness for a brighter future.

    We are ready for joy,

    We are ready for love,

    We are ready for new beginnings.

Amen!

Winter

I refuse to wish away the winter.

It is a glorious season of the year and not simply a prelude to spring.

The winter air is pure and refreshing.

The winter sky has a clarity and brilliance at night.

The winter trees are pencilled in the dawn and sunset.

The winter birds give shows of strength and endurance.

The winter fields hide rare and mysterious truths.

The winter winds sweep friends and family together.

The winter snow invites fun, sport, and play.

The winter ice calls for skill and alertness.

The winter cold inspires hugs and cuddling.

The winter needs elicit gifts and sharing.

The winter silence assists in thought and meditation.

The winter kitchen has deeper smells and finer tastes.

The winter fog and darkness stir joy and merrymaking.

I refuse to wish away the winter.

It is a season rich in meaning and pregnant with the colossus of hope.

Aphorisms

~

Doubt is the shadow of truth.

I prefer an ethical atheist to a slothful theist.

Religion is the only intellectual discipline that glories in stagnation.

Sailing in the wrong direction is sometimes the best way home.

The great fruit of individualism has decayed into the mush of self-infatuation.

Only blushing assures that we see our mistakes, correct our vision, and go on in the ceaseless struggle to be decent.

If I never lose, I am probably not playing in significant games.

Our salvation lies in acknowledging imperfection, then proceeding to crawl forward together.

Humility

I have learned to trust those who are witnesses rather than gurus, those who express their confusion as well as their knowledge, and those who share their suffering along with their joy.

Relaxing

~

Somewhere, in the deep recesses of the soul,
there is a bird singing.

Slow down, listen to the call, and hail the
advent of hope.

Popularity

To escape the trap of public acclaim, an authentic church should advertise as follows:

Our worship is not an entertainment.

Our congregation is not an audience.

Our music is not a concert performance.

Our preaching is not a trivial comfort.

Our theology is not a marketing strategy.

Our counseling is not a promise of prosperity.

Our church is not a business enterprise.

Our ministry is not a cult of personality.

Our community is not a gathering of sheep.

Our success is not a membership statistic.

In fact, it is probably better to be disliked, offensive, and scandalous. Even booing is preferable to mass applause. For no vision is worthwhile without the risk of rebuke. Every truth is born out of painful criticism. Love, itself, is crucifying.

Endings

~

Our kitten was six weeks old, a self-confident little creature, with a know-it-all personality. On the first day out-of-doors, he ran toward a tree, lunged onto the trunk, and began to climb in a vertical direction. Quickly, he went ten feet, twenty feet, thirty feet, fifty feet, until his paws could no longer find a hold. For the rest of the day and night, he clung to a small branch, unable to go up or down and crying for deliverance.

Since the tree was close to the house, I was inspired by an idea for rescue, a specialty of the ministerial profession. Putting a ladder against the garage, I climbed onto the roof, a difficult maneuver while carrying a long board on the shoulder. When I reached the top of the house, I extended the plank across to the tree, sweetly encouraging the kitten to walk. He slowly crawled to safety.

Later, after the family alluded to my mental stability and something about a broken neck, I thought of the little kitten. He was programmed to run, jump, and climb. It is natural to a cat, a survival mechanism. But he did not know that a tree has a top, that it comes to an end. It was a hard lesson to swallow, yet it was a vital piece of knowledge. Now, I notice, ten feet is the maximum climb. Caution, too, is an aspect of survival.

Praying

∼

I love to pray, to go deep down into the silence:

> To strip myself of all pride, selfishness, and
> coldness of heart;
>
> To peel off thought after thought, passion after
> passion, till I reach the genuine depths of all;
>
> To remember how short a time ago I was nothing,
> and in how short a time again I will not be here;
>
> To dwell on all joys, all ecstasies, all tender
> relations that give my life zest and meaning;
>
> To peek through a mystic window and look upon
> the fabric of life—how still it breathes, how
> solemn its march, how profound its perspective;
>
> And to think how little I know, how very little,
> except the calm, calm of the silence, and the
> singing, singing in the night.

Prayer is the soul's intimacy with God, the ultimate kiss.

A Scot's Blessing

~

I hope you have a touch of cynicism:

   a little anger,

   a little gloom,

   a little scorn,

   a little petulance,

   a little denunciation,

   a little derision—

but springing from a noble dream.

Good Dying

~

I believe in good dying.

> Good dying is the recognition of death as natural, necessary, and inevitable. It is a serene understanding of the laws of the universe.

> Good dying is the acceptance of oneself as whole, worthy, and complete. It is a stamp of approval for a life well lived.

> Good dying is leaving the world with honor, grace, and integrity. It is maintaining the dignity of body and character.

That is why every day is a preparation for the end, and why every end should be a reflection of all the days that have gone before. Good living and good dying are a single, healthy stream.

So be it.

A Time to Be Silent

~

There must be a time when we cease speaking
    to be fully present with ourselves.

There must be a time when we exclude clamor
    by listening to nothing whatsoever.

There must be a time when we forgo our plans
    as if we had no plans at all.

There must be a time when we abandon conceits
    and tap into a deeper wisdom.

There must be a time when we stop striving
    and find the peace within.

Amen!